ANIMAL SOUL

ALSO BY BOB HICOK

Plus Shipping

The Legend of Light

ANIMAL SOUL

poems by

BOB HICOK

CONTEMPORARY CLASSICS POETRY SERIES
INVISIBLE CITIES PRESS • MONTPELIER, VERMONT

for
Eve

Invisible Cities Press
50 State Street
Montpelier, VT 05602
www.invisiblecitiespress.com

Library of Congress Cataloging-in-Publication Data

Hicok, Bob, 1960–
Animal soul / Bob Hicok.
cm. – (Contemporary classics poetry series)
ISBN 0-9679683-8-0 (cloth : alk. paper)
ISBN 1-931229-11-2 (paper : alk. paper)
I. Title. II. Series.

PS3558.I28 A8 2001
811'.54—dc21 2001016613

Printed in Canada

Book design by
Peter Holm
Sterling Hill Productions

FIRST PAPERBACK EDITION

CONTENTS

I

II

III

IV

"The name of those fabulous animals (pagan, I regret to say) who used to sing in the water, has quite escaped me." Mr. George Chuzzlewit suggested "Swans." "No," said Mr. Pecksniff. "Not swans. Very like swans, too. Thank you." The nephew . . . propounded "Oysters." "No," said Mr. Pecksniff, . . . "nor oysters. But by no means unlike oysters; a very excellent idea; thank you, my dear sir, very much. Wait. Sirens! Dear me! sirens, of course."

— Charles Dickens,
Martin Chuzzlewit

Cave canem

I

Whither Thou Goest

Fish can have mad cow disease and I have a problem
with that. Purity suffers and salmon can't
moo can't paw grass with the furious
strokes the essential bovine
faith that there's something in the earth
for everyone. All along I've wanted
the good days to be the good days and not
good from twelve to three not
good like drilling your teeth is good
when it stops but good like moonlight
on my wife's hip with the sheets
pulled back and her hair riotous
and misconstrued. That's one thing
and not another. That's the best use
of a bed and two bodies working out
the most inclusive form of redemption
known in the universe this side
of black holes, which is where I want
to be considering that on the other side
of black holes fish with mad cow disease
are indistinguishable from Komodo dragons
who play power forward in the NBA. I'm not
ashamed to admit my prayers are no longer
unconscious but loud and practiced
to the skin of the mirror to the muse
of the cereal box to the road as I drive
everywhere trying to find the last 3/8"
drill this city has because I don't
believe in god but trust that pushing
veneration through my body makes god
exist if only for a second
within the chambered nuances of breath.
In my favorite prayer I apologize for not
having shouted earlier and in public say
from the back of the subway the top
of a table in a Fort Worth bar that *whither*
thou goest I will follow. This should be said
every day and with no substitutions
for the archaic *whither* which is the tender
part the broken wheel of the phrase. This
should be repeated like the turbulence

of blood repeats harmonically or at least
until it's understood that even
if the way things are becomes the way
they are not I'll be there when mad cows
attack when madder fish swim back
through the streams when a black hole
shows up at the door wearing a tie
and promising to suck all dirt all evil
all manner of woe from this life
and smiling in a fashion that breaks
your knees. Whither or when thou goest,
how and why you flee, in what manner
or mode you glide or thrash
there's the mercy of the bond,
there's the moment you wake or refuse
to ever sleep again, there's still
your face when the wind's so fat it curls
in the field to lick its wounds,
and my promise to be there, conspicuously mad
in my devotion.

—•—•—•—

To the Moon, Alice

Last night the man next door tried to throw the woman
next door with an emphasis more on distance
than accuracy while she dug something
of a Marianas Trench in his back that was not

as deep but redder than the original of which
I've seen color-enhanced Landsat photos. Who decides
whether blue's more important than orange
as a conveyance of depth or if the man next door

should continue in that capacity or be promoted
to the con in the next cell who sings Roy Orbison
badly? By this morning some progress
had been made in the arena of these decisions

based on the logic that if two people
of murderous intent are stored in a tight space
over a long period of time they must
eventually learn to select the floral pattern

in something approaching domestic accord. Today
a flurry of Florence Nightingale behavior
includes kisses for the bruise and cut
and the forehead behind which the image

of the chair lifted and bottle thrown still
flares with that nagging incapacity of memory
to rewrite terror as grace. For her there will be
roses, lamb stew with stunted potatoes

and crystallized garlic for him and for both a case
of beer will christen the days when *thank you*
honey it's time for your distemper shot
dear is just a pinch of the treacle they'll stun

each other with. Other inevitables are gravity
and dirt and the resurgence of an ineffective
radical left in American politics to give
the majorities in Durham and Omaha

something to wipe off their boots each November.
There will come another Saturday night
when a section of drywall's confirmed
to be less durable than Samsonite

and the tenacity of hair's proven by foot-pounds
of torque or some fashion of metal
enters flesh at one of the dainty junctures,
after which a judge will instruct a jury to ignore

the defense attorney's allusions to passion
and just focus on the law. For now he's back
and bandaged and mowing, she's inside
and singing to the sewing machine as repairs

continue, I'm at my desk and the trees are poised
for eventual collapse and love is what they feel
and love is what they defend and what
but love follows the corpse to the lovely grave?

Sorting the Entanglements

In my will the basement goes to the spiders. This includes
all the tools and boxes saved for box emergencies.
Particularly the Shop Vac cannot be touched. The Shop Vac
can kill more spiders per second than any device short

of a bomb. Bombs are messy whereas Shop Vacs were designed
for people who fear lint and want to vacuum water. From water
came the trout with no eyes. My friend Tom suggested we clean
the trout and cook it in butter and have it on the table

when my wife came home. We would be smiling at the trout
with no eyes and she'd eat some of the trout with no eyes
and be impressed with our small competency. I asked Tom
if he was troubled by this ocular deficiency. He asked me

if I'd intended to eat the eyes. Tom left with the trout
and feeling sick to his stomach. I'd have to kill the spiders
to discover if they still have eyes. Because my basement's
a Wildlife Preserve, I'd go to jail for that. My dream date

doesn't begin with the question, *What'cha in for, boy?*
The trout's part of a larger sadness including three-legged
elk and impotent sperm whales. For those of you who scan
rather than read, that's impotent and not important. Important

sperm whales apparently don't exist. I too feel small
before these facts and prefer a game of Jarts to environmental
activism. Jarts, while dangerous, can be played without slogans
and bullhorns and placards, you need a lawn and beer

and the willingness to impale or be impaled. In short we all
qualify. I admire the spiders even as I fear them. They knit
their homes straight out of their bodies. If I did this
I'd have a home made of vomit and piss. The only people

who'd visit would be people I'd rather not know. Time
and again the pattern of spiderwebs comes out the same.
I can't write my name twice without fooling myself as to who
I am. I believe this ability of spiders constitutes some kind

of wisdom. I believe this is what the I.M.F. calls miraculous.
In the next county, Herefords give birth to fibroid tumors,
peltless minks are the rage in France. *Oops* is not a big enough
word. *Sorry* is not. *Stupid* begins to exploit the lexicon.

I enjoy the image of a lawyer reading my will to the spiders.
The spiders are shitting their webs and stacking flies. The new owners
must negotiate access to the fuse box. I bequeath my snow tires
to the hyacinth. I leave my body to the unfashionable Earth.

—•—•—•—

Vagina canticle

One woman who was seventy-two had never seen her vagina . . . She said it took her over an hour, because she was arthritic by then, but when she finally found her clitoris, she said, she cried.

—Eve Ensler

Healed by water
her hand unfolds, fingers uncurl to ancient
length, slow
as coral awakens, Bach in the room, Bach

sliding up and down pink tiles,
on her breath the light
from candles

runs away, fingers
extended, if you've never
seen a gondola a gondola

amazes, never tasted salt

your own skin is a feast, one lick's
a harvest
of the body,

the soft message of her fingers
is new, warm
as the water, there's time, Bach

isn't going anywhere, candles patiently eat
their shadows,
if you found a butterfly inside your ear,

roused a dream
sleeping inside your dream, you
might cry, and she unearths

a thriving tree
with born-again hands,
there's a piano in the room, music

in the water, and skin gathered
is ungathered,

a place of singular moment, and she alone
touches where she alone
exists, 72 is a good

year, decades without, a life
without deliberate pleasure

hones

pleasure, you might cry, quick breaths
now, and beyond
the little gasps, shudders of flesh

unfurled, there's suddenly
a cryptic
self, a deeper
echo, and every day

there's water, Bach's lush
revelation, and each morning the sun,
each night a candle,

this spot around which
her broken fingers
turn green.

—•—•—•—

Birth of a Saint

If there's a gun in her theory of Heaven it's unloaded,
pearl-handled, graced with the feel of flesh
extending from hand to steel, the confidence
of her palm radiating to the man
behind the counter and converting sullen
to smile, making him wet, making him stammer that she
can have anything she wants, bounty of Slim Jims
& Newports, all the cocks in all the Playgirls
and enough money to make her car zoom
across the whisper of Kansas and Nebraska.
Even as she flees, her Impala moving from 80 to 100
to 127 at full stride, the gun's weight, the drop-forged
mass would hold her down, keep her moving
through mists of Del Shannon and Nirvana,
she could think back to the Twelve
Interlocking Lectures on Heaven, could remember
the SUNY professor speaking to the bulb
of the microphone as he said *Heaven is not a place*
but the refusal of place, not a wish
but the ability to confuse all wishes. This
would allow her to close her eyes and will
away the State Troopers' triangulation, evade
the appetite of law-enforcement technology. This
would compel her to meditate a second body,
a third self, to drive to the desert, to count
the broken grains of sand and kiss every scorpion
full on the lips they don't have. This is what
dopamine and the synaptic cleft and too much
Scoobie Doo made of her thoughts in the few
seconds after she asked for a pack
of Beemens and was basically ignored
basically spit at by the clerk if we can spit
with our eyes didn't Ollie North
sit in the senate sending fuck-you
vibes laced with dribble out to our little
screens. And that she says nothing but thank you
when he finally moves his hands in the pattern
we call making change: that she doesn't
kick the Hostess display or cop a few dozen
Bazooka Joes: that even her dreams of revenge

have her holding an unloaded gun:
have her thinking please be kind please
let there be dignity in the small moments
grace in the graceless acts let me live
through this day not wanting to hate
not wanting to kill: that she wonders
driving away in her cloud of a car
if she didn't do something wrong if there isn't
something cataclysmic in her face something
offensive in the architecture of her nose
makes her a saint a stupid saint a saint
who'll get no holiday no entry in the Emerald
Book of Saints so you and I must agree
on a name that she'll be known
as the Stop-n-Go Saint the Burger King
Saint that as we wait in line we'll grind
our teeth in prayer tap our feet in homage
that when we lean in and grab
a fist of shirt a fist of hair and scream
give me the goddamn burger now we'll say
please we'll chant thank you we'll pick up
our condiments and slip them neatly
into the trash.

—•—•—•—

Everyday Commerce

The hand wanted money so the body could take a bus
to Kalamazoo. The hand is famous in these parts
for holding itself shakily in the air as the mouth
points out that the hand is missing two fingers.

The woman who owns the mouth further confessed
that her daughter's daughter sleeps
in a Kalamazoo hospital with a few machines
saying *puck-wheeze-puck* beside her infirm

soul desperate for the three-finger touch
of her Grandma Rose. Grandma Rose didn't remember
that two years ago she rang my bell
like a rabid piece of Berlioz and panted

about Lansing and her son's left leg
and a chainsaw and *could I would I of course*
I'll pay you back. That Grandma Rose stuttered
whereas this Grandma Rose stuttered more.

That Grandma Rose smelled of coffee grounds
whereas this Grandma Rose smelled of the landfill
built around the legacy of coffee grounds. She
had brown skin in the sense we all do except

albinos, who in their seeming delicacy
are terrestrial incarnations of jellyfish.
Her brown skin seemed more translucent after years
of abrasion by the circuits of the moon. This

is everything I can do to suggest the concept
of Grandma Rose. From here it's all commentary,
whether I gave money or not, if she danced to my yes
or spit at my no, whether I understand need

as a lion trainer's whip or the feathers
in my pillow as I search the night for sleep. Let's
assume kindness vestigial, a tail we flick
that's a memory of holding further sway with the air.

Let's admit what we own is a sacrament,
a bond between our slumping flesh and the inevitable
earth. Now choose between propositions. This is why
I hate Ann Landers and Pat Robertson, they advise

not to stab the host with the little fork or eat
human flesh on the sabbath, remaining otherwise
mute on matters of concern to myself and Grandma Rose
as we stood in my living room, one nodding,

one stammering about a body coming apart a few hours
away, both knowing the bodies are coming apart
here and faster than we can extend our hands
and lie about how easy it is to fill them.

How Origami was Invented

The last I went to confession was to whisper
I like being alone. I was penanced to sing
Stayin' Alive one hundred times. Solitude
almost tastes like grapes, of course not
but alone I can think such things,
there's no one to counter *strawberries.*
Particularly the Big Holidays are a good time
to have a conversation with buildings,
everyone's gone, to talk with buildings
you merely lean against them,
they do the rest, brick is thrilled
to be touched, marble, I shun marble, so
haughty. Cities need to be alone and oceans
and the moon gets too much credit
lets leave it out of this. I've been given
vast sympathy for this affliction.
Did you know the face of someone who thinks
you're a loser
slash
psychotic looks like a photo of Nixon
lifted from newspaper with Silly Putty
and stretched? While thinking of that sentence
remember this isn't a science.
If I was not alone sometimes I'd all the time
not want to be with people. This
because we invented spandex and chitchat.
Other species invent beehives and asexual
reproduction and spots on wings that look
like eyes but are just spots.
Sometimes I wish the mouth
looked like the mouth but was just the mouth
being kissed. The mouth
kissed both presents and works against
solitude. If that idea was origami
I'd refold it into a heron. I can't, not yet,
but I'm alone this weekend and there's paper
everywhere on which I've tried
to write a clear path to you.

Harms Way

Inevitable death and our agony to attain Utopia have made existence a form of pathology.

—Joel-Peter Witkin in *Harms Way,* a book of photographs

Look.   Look away.

Picture

of alligator boy versus actual
blue sky,
the nodular lesions of late syphilis
are not unlike clouds

as disgust is not wholly removed
from rapture. To be

enthralled. A face

ripped open, flesh and bone
hung from the surgeon's rigging, masked

face of the Paisley girl, skin
of palmettes, woman's face

with hole in nose, face
of child with no brain, face

of woman wielding whip,
smoking as her chained

lover grovels, her corseted boredom
erotic.   Look.

Look away. I lose the book
for a year, find it in a closet, make

tea, walk my dog. Open it
and stare out the window. Blue
sky, clouds

make me think of eschatologies,
the impossibility
of casting final shapes, of christening

anomalies. I look
for the naked woman
curled on a love seat with her toe

in the nose of a skeleton so I might

better describe,
might say
I look away and the light has changed,

a winter prerogative, might admit

I'd have no questions for her
if we met, I'd shun her, walk away and yet

months later, hours
later, turn to this page, these
bones, and find nothing strange because here

it is, and find the moment brutal
because here it is. Sepia

pubic hair, sepia smile, sepia nipple
occluded. Look.

Look away. *Lust & madness, murder & mayhem* —
black words
impressed on a black cover. Sepia

pages like something
lightly burnt, singed

skin, and flesh coming apart
on every page, and the shadows, the death shroud

of forgiveness.

—•—•—•—

Neither Here nor There

Again with the gunfire, vague pops that suggest
we live in a bowl of Rice Krispies. The Earth

moves at 18 miles per second and the sound
clings, the sound travels as if menace were clawed.

Here it is at my door, knocking, being upstaged
by the more evolved gunfire on TV. Kids ask

Why don't we slip off, not knowing we do. Kids
ask older kids how to release the safety, reload,

when to shoot. Always is one common answer.
The gunfire's there, I am here. Here and there

are words I've forgotten in German, I even knew
for an afternoon how to say to a small boy

in French, *I am a teapot, short and stout, here
is my handle, there is my spout.* That small boy

laughed, which is the service French provides
when administered by an American tongue. Pluto

moves at 3 miles per second though without
benefit of gunfire. Maybe everyone's shooting

at Pluto because it blocks our view of eternity.
Maybe a hole in a body is the equivalent

of a conference on Derrida, a way of exchanging
information, a way of breaking everything down

into bite-size, into blood-soaked bits. Here
becomes more there all the time. For instance

the growth of bars on windows like crystals
in a beaker after a catalyst is introduced.

Catalyst fear. Catalyst the bleeding of money
to and fro. Here green trees make a tent,

the density of the Earth is 344 pounds per cubic
foot, lawnmowers debate each other on Saturdays

and guns are pets. Everything's the same
there except leisure is hunger

and hunger the artifact of an unflinching
weather. Slowly the dead kids there

matriculate into the dead kids here. This
is progress if you consider that graves

are no longer dug by hand or caskets lowered
by wailing relatives, instead motors are used,

instead a backhoe grumbles through a few
ravenous bites. Then a chunk of stone's

thrown down that was cut from the zooming Earth,
the heavy Earth, then someone chisels

Here Lies and we go home and listen to the sky
chatter like the rivets are popping out.

Rapture

In a bathroom lit by a 25-watt bulb the blue
genitals from a Bic fine-point look
like cave paintings in Lascaux only less
articulate. I'm standing where and doing
what you'd expect after four
cognacs I drank as reminders
of Sarajevo and the idea I once had
I could travel so far even my whispers
would be interpreted as the rapture
of a man speaking in tongues. Recognize
the cinematic present tense: I say
I'm zipping, flushing now, enjoying
the swim of my thoughts as I approach
a table burned with initials
and swastikas and nod to a woman
with a scar from a bear
on her thigh. Even though I'm not. Even
though I'm in a room with little light,
a few pictures of love on the desk
and pop-out man on the wall
showing me everything he's made of,
the red parts, the blue tubes
that carry promises from heart to brain.
In the bar I'm asking the woman how
she escaped or if she looked
back at the steam rising from her trail
of blood on snow. She doesn't say
if her soul slipped through her teeth
and flickered like an aurora, an inquisition
of light she followed to camp
and morphine and dreams
chased by a breath she only wanted to touch.
She does order another drink. She does
begin to sound more and more like a teletype
machine, and cries until I order
another drink and cry
with her, not understanding why
until later, until staring at the pictures
on the desk and the man cut open to the psalm
of his bones. When we drink

enough we become Escher holding a ball,
looking at stairs and seeing how they go
every- and nowhere at once, the events
of our lives compress to singularity,
to one night in one room with one voice
screaming through the telephone
that the moon is in the carport
Mozart's on the patio and love is yours
right now but here I am getting ready
to take it away. So she spoke
of the bear and her mother and dropping
out of college as if all words
were one word, all loss the same
unweaving of a tapestry by distracted hands.
I interpreted the dream of killing my boss
as really a dream of killing my father
which is secretly a wish to kill myself,
confessed that my ambition to die
is ultimately a need to be reborn
and that the soul reborn is a hawk
that circles one
needless time before descending
to the sparrow. None of which
I want cut on my death-stone or read back
by a stenographer in court as I try
to channel my embarrassment into renewed
powers of invisibility, just as the next time
I saw this woman she looked down
at her shoes as if her feet were trying
to get away but smiled when she looked up,
much as she smiles now over my shoulder,
remembering what it was like to mean everything
you have no idea you're saying.

—•••—

Ha'ish hu ha'ish

> *. . . the following cable was sent . . . Ha'ish hu ha'ish. The nearest English translation is "The man is the man."*
>
> *. . . and the ashes were scattered over the waters of the Mediterranean. This was the end of Adolf Eichmann.*
>
> —*The Capture and Trial of Adolf Eichmann*

The man is ash in his hands. Eight miles out,
water of no country, the rhythm of the boat

inside his body and the boat obeying the sea.
He breathes salt but remembers the kapo's
licorice breath, spiteful stench of turnips

as the white roots turned black in piles
across the compound. He saw the man once

in his Benz, lambent eyes, Botticelli lips,
a dissonant grace within the machine of Belsen.
The sky's pricked with stars, water mumbles

against the boat, the choked words of a woman
with gas in her throat. He pours what remains

of Eichmann through each hand, wanting to touch
the disappearance, to be sure what vanishes
is the cloud of the man and not the dream

of revenge. So little, he thinks, three pounds
of fluff he measures against the mounds

he was made to stare at from his knees. Coming
back, no one speaks against the motor's single word.
Tel Aviv is waking, children shout after balls

as their shadows dust streets. There's a lightness
to his flesh, the sensation he can rise

from himself, out of his body's custody of death,
as he walks slowly home, unaware he carries
the devil's ashes under the nails of his hands.

What Fine Kindling the Homeless Make

I know the importance of replication but intend no action
in this regard. For instance Descartes removed the eye
of an ox and scraped and looked through the back
of this eye and realized the world was upside down.

Doing this once is enough because the body knows
intuitively the world is upside down. The body knows
having the eye removed is not volitional in the sense
I'll have fries with that is, you can put ketchup on fries

or salt, leave them untouched on a white plate as a woman
explains it's the addition of rare-earth elements
to bronze that makes the statues appear robust. Before
entering the restaurant's neon euphoria, this woman and I

walked by an alley where a different experiment had been
repeated. Participants in this investigation tend to live
a few days with tubes, little Niles ferrying fluids in
and hope out of their bodies, they spew unfashionable amounts

of puss and say incoherent things that sound like French
pared of everything but the full glottal stop. Apparently
once isn't enough when the lure of ten awaits, when
gasoline's available at reasonable prices and no two people

burn in precisely the same manner or with screams
of equally operatic worth. I remain open to possibilities.
The iron maiden may have been necessary to the development
of the PosturePedic. I might open a book at random

to a passage about St. Augustine opening a book at random.
The burning of strangers is potentially a ritual in the New
Pilgrimage, a way of bending the knee, of worshiping
creation by proving its simplicity by means of simple

erasure. What do I know of science, what in the art
of the species has revealed itself sincerely to my socketed
eyes, I'm not one to ask about the tempering of bronze
so it looks more startled, not one to contest

the incendiary delights. I propose to repeat this experiment
every day: breathe. Otherwise initial conditions
are what Gods paint on the boring orbs, otherwise
indignation is a tiresome song. How brightly the bodies

burn and for what purpose is not a sacrament at my disposal.
Breathe. We don't notice what we think we do, said
my friend of the New Hampshire license plate he edited
into *Live Free and Die*. This might mean the burned

were not burned at all but elevated to the astrum,
that everyday-low-price is a prayer, a delusion,
perhaps our sparse and mumbled outrage is a way
of saying in the manner of a child, do it again.

The Subjects' Exodus

Life is not that lifelike.
—Susan Sontag

We were children in the painting, ran
through the mist of wheat,
blue-capped, demonically apple-cheeked,
our joy
inventing the caked sunlight, each
nervous brush-stroke
suggesting the violence of our contentment.

We grew into the snobs & soot-nosed
of the novel, men
who held their best conversations
with machines,
women versed in the theology of hats, all
transparent, our bones just
clothes racks for the novelist,
who died
after a vigorous pursuit
of rapture through syphilis.

In the song we were angelic
in the hippest sense,
incapable of miracles but prophets
of their necessity,
discovered the nervous system's
a star map, lyricized sex
and the pharmacological
side effects of love
to a baseline, Fender and carpet of drums.

In the poem we were given words in clumps,
less song
than porridge, made to fly
through paintings and stare
at dreams,
to tearfully remember
each thing
we'd once remembered:
we died philosophically, the poet

making cute his necropheliac tendencies,
the affairs he carried on
with the dead, always claiming
it was the soul's
stark chronicle he was after
when his heart was fixed
on the seduction of a grant.

We'll not be back.
What's drawn is drawn, said
said. Paint silence, sculpt
no one's face.
We recognize alone
these Muses: Fear and Love
and Bread.
Your work will proceed
unabated:
you never did cherish us.

—•—•—•—

Perpetual Resurrection

Enough snow for tracks and blood, enough moon to imply
that light's everlasting, a grace of the abiding
sky. He pounded, bruised the door with a child's

impractical fists, his feet bare and Pooh on his chest,
Pooh with a paw in the jar and the jar labeled honey
and my friend's pajamas falling down. My mother and father

on the stairs, whispering like saws in the distance,
running down like rain eager to touch, to cover
the forgotten earth. Now I can say the marks on his back

were the same as Van Daniken's arrows and landing
strips, signs of visitations, etchings of gods
who leave maps for other gods, whose art can only be

monumental. Can say they were beautiful, filaments of red
against the prosody of white, almost the pattern of a flag,
nearly a theory of semiotics. At the time they were simply

what attracted my mother's hands, wounds she washed,
welts she tended with the same care she gave food
and clothes, her face unfolding, easing into the domestic

ministry, a love for the work that must be done.
And there was the dance between my father and the man
who ran in, tumbling and a spray of arms, shouts

and the walls assaulted, a plant crushed and our dachshund
growling, hacking as if the moon was stuck in her throat.
After they left, the boy carried away in one arm, limp

as felt, after solace and explanation, after 30 years
my friend's gone through seven lives and is constructing
an eighth: a new city, clothes fresh from Milan, a sudden

passion for Augustine and quartz, the floor of his loft
a maze of agates and cherts through which he weaves
his devotion to obstacle. Days after the beating

there was a hammer and river, he spent hours
trying to batter water to a stop, driving rocks into mud,
forcing earth into earth, a mouth swallowing itself.

And the small maple behind him dying because he was in love
with the sound it made, the heart it boasted
when he attacked, the hammerhead flattening, the claw

tearing out great veins of wood, cluttering dirt
with splintered flesh. Then his left hand placed flat
on a boulder, the hammer lifted and brought down,

his stare the first time, the second, by the third
he was looking at a premonition in the shadows
of a copse. Everyone asks about the scars and he says

the cable holding a coil of steel snapped, a car
slipped off a jack. I believe the moon fell and he
tried to catch it, that denial's undervalued

as a martial art, I nod, sip my drink and worship
the weather until it's late enough that not
even waitresses pretend they hold each moment dear.

—•—•—•—

Magic

Mirrors, it's all done
with mirrors.

Mirrors and scalpel,
hormones at first, medroxy-
progesterone and a floral print
dress, little

roses, little roses and white
gloves. Hormones
at first, a short walk
as a woman, floral
print dress, white gloves, just down

to the Piggly Wiggly in nylons
and pumps. Not
enough, still
the clustered flesh between his legs,
still the stroked

rush of blood, ten times, fifteen times a day
he'd masturbate, *I have become*
the serpent
in his journal, it's all done

with mirrors. When doctors
wouldn't
he did, mirrors and scalpel and his own
hands, orchiectomy is a bloodless

word, the clustered flesh
cut away, his hands
in the mirrors and not
enough. The wounds

healed, the scars almost resembled
a vagina, he almost believed his body
a woman's, hormoned
breasts, floral print
dress, white gloves, almost felt

calm, there was nothing left to touch

but in dream, in his journal
he was still a man, *I moved*
to the back of the bus but could still
smell her cunt,
her clitoris pointed at me, it had a halo,

my hands are not done. And then

scalpel, mirrors,
a cut below the wings of the ribs,
abdomen
opened, seven hours of blood, routing

for the adrenals, kidney
retracted, the pain too much,

in his journal he'd copied
Matthew, *And if your hand*
or your foot
causes you to stumble, cut it off and throw it
from you. Below the wings

of ribs, a crooked line, red wish,
his body pulled
inside out, the skin drawn back, wings
of a dove, seven hours

and still the body of a man,
hope and blood
run out, and mirrors, they never love you
enough.

—•—•—•—

Finally I Buy X-ray Glasses

At 13 I questioned when it would stop, this
seeing through. Wouldn't my supercharged glance
invade walls and blouses and bones, pierce
to atoms and smaller still, even pass
through the film of the soul as it tunneled
to the scowling mask of God, leaving me blind
for the sin of snooping flesh? I was a literalist
who believed secrets were solved inside, that
any mystery, even lust, could be taken apart,
pieces sifted down to the blessing of the whole.
That was before the burn of your face at dusk
across the wooden table, something more
than your body in the moment's text, light
turned to skin, to words that circled the room
like the shadows of birds: before you moved
from dresser to bed, your flesh a vestige
of candlelight, every need, all love born
to the surface, a radiance I could touch.
Last night I came home to a box
from the Johnson Smith Company, X-ray Specks
and arcana describing how to keep
their Zeus-power in check. What began
as a laugh became kisses that chased us
into bed. You wore the glasses,
I closed my eyes and felt you
                                                                                watching me
thinking of you
                                                        looking through me
as I stared back, which is exactly
what making love should be like.

—•—•—•—

The Party

Bugs are chewed by the blue light into something
like the excrement of ghosts. We are still
drinking at 40 for the same reasons as 21
only our shirts are better, our hands
are less inclined to destroy the elegant
shrubbery, now we own
the elegant shrubbery and suckle it
on Saturdays before the ascent
of white balls dimpled for aero-dynamic
zest. Finally there's no shame
in drinking domestic wine, it's a matter
of degree, of vintner and how much,
the ratio between pâté and chardonnay,
sip and chug, and do your gestures
become menacing like a windmill
or trenchant like the chop-chop of Julia
Child? At 21 a car was necessary
for the mobility of its loneliness
and the basic philosophy of speed, zoom
goes the head, zoom the body and why not
peppermint Schnapps, why not blotter
together with the shattered stars,
and when hips were involved, when
two mouths whispered along the pinker
joints of flesh, the river drummed
its broken fingers, the shards of glass
cultivated by gravel stared at the moon
with the moon's own eyes. At 40
a well-moored veranda's better backdrop
for rapture, maybe three drinks, maybe
by the fifth someone will remember
the rudiments of dancing, another
will begin to eat her napkin, just
nibbling as she talks of the chalks
she put away, the notebooks
she used to fill with bodies that looked
like anemones praised by an updraft
of wind. Bugs perish until someone
throws a hamburger at the light
and the light goes nova and thereafter

mosquitos find the booming veins
wherein the sustaining music flows.
What we see of each other in the dark
is what fish at the core of the ocean
make a pact with, so much movement,
the gestures of creatures
slowly abraded by the fluid
that gives them life. This is when
someone begins a song we all know
but can't fully remember, when new verses
are invented that bear the shape
of the original but move lurch-stop
like crutches, like tumbleweeds
taking an inventory of the bruised land.

Critique of Pure Unreason

If I meant to be taken literally I'd have a bigger body,
better breath, the voice of a vice so the bones
of strangers would be easier to hold, easier to channel

into stocks or whatever water-sports my literal self
deems relevant for minions. A bald-headed
man should be figurative, if he mentions

a box-end wrench in a conversation about Husserl,
you should know he does so because he can't say Husserl,
box-end wrench is easier to pronounce and therefore

a better foundation for philosophy, even an out-of-body
experience becomes a practical thing when your spirit
holds something from Craftsman in its wispy hand.

Yesterday I was a bald-headed man caught
in a conversation with a short and mostly adorable,
mostly literal Hungarian, it was his three-beer rant,

an intricate Rube Goldberg thing he constructs with bits
of Auschwitz and the World Bank, Stalin gets mentioned
in honorific tones some reserve for Mickey Mantle,

where is an out-of-body experience when you need it,
what did Husserl ever write about Hungarians
who believe Roosevelt was Satan and Jews

have one testicle, what recourse but metaphor
in the form of a steel pipe, what reasoned breath
can you throw at an eighty-year-old man

whose smile out-performs the moon when he leans
back and says *the ovens, now there was a good start?*
I've entirely given up on the idea that when I enter

a room certain parts of the brains of the people
already in that room will make the calculations
that allow them to think, a body has just entered

the room. If the woman wearing Dior was to look
directly at my blue eyes and say to all
gathered in the voice of Winston Churchill, *a spaceship*

has just entered the room, sell your bonds,
wrap your heads in tin-foil, I'd have to say yes,
that's entirely possible, it would explain

that run-down feeling I've had. Because you can't
listen to someone you love place other people
you love in the context of vermin, can't try

the 75th time to apply reason in the way it should be
used, which is very much like a box-end wrench,
very much in the tradition of words meaning what words

mean, of *love* as love and *hate* as that which love
subdues, can't do anything but say: you're right,
and a straight line can be drawn between the technology

of human sacrifice and the invention of the cotton-gin—
it's not out of the question that ATMs scan our souls
and feed digitized bio-luminescence to a Cray

in Tel Aviv programmed to eradicate the grace
and snappy rituals of Christianity: or good night,
my usual choice, good night and I'll see you later,

we'll talk some other time, maybe in another life, maybe
on the moon, maybe next time I'll leave my head
on the kitchen table, maybe we can stand in the backyard

and reminisce about Eden, when we didn't exist and nothing
was more cunning, nothing threw a better dinner party
than our ancestors, methane gas and acid rain.

—•—•—•—

Headline: CLEAN-SWEEP CLEARS PARKS & GRATES

She was a stench like dead leaves and sparrows
clotted

beside the river a wound stark as the red palms
of Christ

a saint to pigeons example to none a stench
like roses

too long in the vase corroded by the appetite
of water.

———

Wool coat over wool sweater over parchment
skin weren't enough, she froze in full
sight, in the grip of the moon, changed cell
by cell from a pliant animal of marginal
sense, of sharp utterances like a clash
of horns, like the grinding of stones
in the belly of the Earth, to a statue
of herself, mad-mouth open, eyes printed
with a map of the stars, eyes wide
and swallowing light, devouring the moon.

———

In her cart, decontextualized mall, stainless
        mesh: empty Crayola box, microwave
                door, clothesline and decanter,

rat-chewed bologna and newspapers folded,
        stacked along sides, packed tight
                at the bottom, forming a box,

a crib for the child—lice-haired, crusty-
        eyed, face blue but still a wisp
                of breath, still a cry

when the patrol-woman lifted her up, wrapped
        her coat, wrapped her voice around
                the child, whispering

the nonsense of comfort, coos and clicks
        amounting to pleas, demands
                to flourish, to live.

———

We can walk now in any direction
without her grumbling stench without

the petition of her chapped hands walk
to the store the moon the opera

where the poor sing the seduced sing
where the dying sing so tenderly we cry

and give them our love praise the golden
cavities of their throats which bless

with song which caress in languages
we don't understand with words

that sound like waves splintering
like satin hinges closing like a dying

woman a psychotic woman asking
the sky to take everything back.

—•••—

Pol Pot's Class Reunion

Not everyone with a green thumb can bury a body
with each tree. Some Cambodians did along Rue

Pol Pot and now palms susurrate overhead

where the dead can't hear the swish that gives
purpose to such a beckoning word. I bury
the pinkies of my victims with each Whittier rose

I plant and nurture to red bounty

with show tunes at midnight and all the zinfandel
rhizomes can handle. Some plants sober up

and join AA, some dissent to *South Pacific* and insist
on *Carousel,* I tire of roses and have begun

an affair with daffodils. This alone could get me

killed, or my misunderstanding of the term
revolutionary cadre, there'll come a time

when blue eyes alone destine my body for the top
of the pile. A wizened Pol Pot adjusted

his scarf as two sinuous men held him up, led
the old legs, feathery torso away. House arrest,
the reporter said, and I question what the house

did, knowing how evil toilets can get. He looked
like my grandfather if my grandfather had been
Cambodian and said yes to many bullets
in the back of many heads. This would have made

for the stunning garden he could never grow.
My grandfather too should have had a show-trial,

a moment to snooze in a chair as his sins were listed
to the zealous shouts of *youza-boss* from a crowd

spontaneously gathered. I myself will confess
if in return my roses are cherished and fed

now and then human remains. This should pose
no problem, given the ratio of supply to demand.

—•—•—•—

33

There's the joke about the inmates who know
the jokes so well they've numbered them
and shout the numbers and everyone goes
ha ha when they hear 12 or 263 but
the new guy hollers 72 and gets no yucks
and is stumped behind his brand-new
super-tough-alloy bars until the arsonist
with the SS Nimitz tattooed to his chest
says *boy it ain't the joke it's how*
you tell it. The first time I heard this
it made me smile made me laugh not so much
because it's a hoot but due to the effect
of a man trying to drink a beer
with his head lying on a table as he told
a joke in basically reverse order except
he gave the punch line twice once
at the start once at the end except
by the time he got to the end he sounded
like a garbage disposal filled with socks.
He drank that beer because the twelve
previous hadn't managed to pull
the moon down on his head or result
in the lobotomy more or less promised
by Westerns in which the psychically
wounded hero goes into town
or curls up with his horse and drinks
himself into a song or a fight and the next
day everything's all right the cameras
are waiting the orchestra is waiting
the Indians are waiting to die his girl's
waiting to swoon and damn it
there's only so much light let's wrap
this puppy. What hadn't gone right for him
is pretty much what hasn't gone right
for me is the same Greek tragedy
you've been wearing for thirty-seven years
like it's the only coat that fits.
What he wanted was love too and money
like you and just like you
some kind of music in the background

that your soul wrote on its best day
while you were impressed by the profile
of trees and not despising
your fat ankles with customary vehemence.
You and I and everyone at the bar
and everyone driving too fast
with the music up and crying and the rest
of the world slumped over papers
and straining on the pot: we should
come up with a list a table of woe
a code we can invoke while passing
on the subway while waiting
for the connecting flight: we should
be able to whisper 92 shout 7 gnash
a string of numbers as long
as the daydreams of computers as complicated
as the truth that the dishes are piling
the electricty's being cut off
there's an Adventist at the door there's poison
in the milk and the one person
who'd listen to your theory that a rope
slung from an elegant branch would more
than support your weight wants the rope
for herself and for exactly
the same reasons only how
she describes them how
she tells the joke how she says
enough involves slightly different
though no less forsaken inflections.

—•—•—•—

Cross Town

She turns to see his thumb on ice.
The subway rides its ocean with familiar
anxiety. The shirt turbaned
to his left hand's alive
if you consider the progress of blood
through cotton a manner of speech.
A circle forms around his body as around
a fire. The boy and the bag
of ice sweat to the struggles
of the boom box at the end
of the car, adrenal thrash
and replicated pattern with slender
variation, iterated beat with a notch
removed here a skip added there
like a vowel like a snarl
from a scar-trimmed throat.
The thumb moves because the train
shakes and she turns away
and back to the blood-plumes
weaving the ice as they drift
from the digit's base and mesh
and feather with the speed of revolution.
Dios mio a man says as he slices
the air with the sign of the cross.
Was Jesus bored by pain? One reflex
to touch the other to run, she rocks
back and forth, her body stammering,
unresolved. At Lexington hats
and briefcases board like an attack
of thrushes. The thumb vanishes, the ice
disappears, the man's Montreaux
T-shirt with its smear of colors
bragging of the impetuous
swirl of jazz are erased by so much
flesh, so many raincoats in a hurry
for the womb of closets. As a whisper
might she touches a shoulder, brushes
a thigh until she stands behind
the man, ambitious but without plan.
The train shakes its hips. She places

a hand flat and wide to his back,
across the pearls of his spine
as they move through a hole
cut through the wounded Earth.

—•—•—•—

A Small Blasphemy

No one in Ibsen kisses when they talk about death
but even the cutlery in *A Doll's House* broods
so strenuously it hums. We are smaller than art

and more nervous, deprived the focus of a cunning
metaphysic but not the huge appetite of our couch,

where we sank after the Memorial in our mismatched
blacks, sleeve against whispering hem, bones
and words batched in collapse after the stiff

fatigue of proper distress. So we kissed and talked
and didn't talk and didn't kiss, for awhile

twined and then apart, this is how continents live,
is fear why the moon makes it clear it's always
ready to hide? I remembered being made to kiss

an uncle, you a grandmother, your body shadowed
by your mother's as you stood in the conga line

of grief, then hoisted, then told to say good-bye
to a lace dress wearing closed eyes. This
is turning a child's head inside out, schooling

hands, lips in a backward faith, a belief
in the *no* that waits inside the husk of promises:

the vow of love, the oath of flesh. If God prefers
we whisper and rend, each kiss was blasphemy,
our souls will be scattered like wrens

inside the appetite of the sky. Yet we kissed
again, bewildered by mourning less carnally dressed.

—•••—

Season of Levitation

My mother's looking for the last
leaf touched by rain so high
if she falls from the oak
my father cannot catch her
the moon will be too late
with its grasp but she wants
to hold her cheek to the most
green the softest green
the world owns the sun
caresses because the dishes
are high in the sink
like mountains pushing up
and the grandchildren already
have children and soon
the last chance to get lost
in the trees will be the wish
she makes inside
her final breath so now
is the time to climb
with hands and feet now
is the hour to let neighbors
call police there is a leaf one
leaf a last leaf the rain
has touched one drop waiting
hanging just to fall into her mouth
to reach everything old

inside that's curled inside
like the most
secretive root a leaf
waits at the top bends
at the top from the weight
the small weight of one
drop of one
world of one last chance
to adore beyond reason

—•—•—•—

An incidental report on my grandmother's divinity

My grandmother had fourteen children,
56 grandchildren, 57 great and one
great-great and a packet
of coffee in her coffin and a love

for the church that anyway had the roof
tarred on the day of her funeral.
She was 87 and weighed
82 pounds and one of her children

asked where the will was and another
did the stations of the cross
for the first time in 32
years, a journey familiar as breath.

The priest performed the Eucharist with arms
outstretched
crucifixion style, the roof boomed
and back-talked and a little girl

with Down's turned in her pew
and smiled combustively. Many men
wore suits and many men
wore jeans, one a Saturn jacket, one

a Buffalo Bills windbreaker
and he didn't kneel at the kneeling
parts, that's optional now, he sat back
and kissed his pink-haired

girlfriend and the roof shook,
stained glass rattled. My grandmother
was a cornucopia, an ocean, from her
sons and daughters flowed, accountants

and junkies, she was responsible
for an Everest of diapers
and remembered all the names
because she was a god, her reflex

was to smile even as her children fought
over her body, the flesh of a few
dollars, she believed in Heaven
as I believe in wing nuts

and the church smelled of tar,
the church saved a few dollars and she
was a god, she said she would die
in six days and did and her children

can fight over loneliness now.
The church can go on its watertight
way, its between the Earth
and my grandmother now, what

the future is, how love is construed,
she and my grandfather will mix
despite their miracle coffins, something
must give to pressure, their trickster

souls will seep out and no one
will know where they go, not
church or children, God or the weather
service, and the chatter of the village

they created will abate as my grandmother
makes a cup of coffee for her husband,
finally they can watch the steam
rise and kiss where the age spots

were, all the ticklish parts
that haven't belonged to them
since the first child emerged to screams
of holy insistence.

Monograph on the Walkers

Because they never talk I infer telepathy
across the short distance, always four,
sometimes five feet but no more, maybe six,
the limit seems to be six as if tethers,
as if invisible arteries connect their bodies
in a better way, with greater infatuation
than speech. He's tall and she's short,
she leans into her stride like a ski jumper,
his head's always about to come off, bounces
as if the bolted vertebrae are loose,
as if of all his possessions it's the least
essential. If he's good at math he uses
the bones of equations as an excuse
to study the scatter of a contrail
across the pudgy face of the moon,
if she's good with her hands she's rebuilding
Atlantis in their bathroom, only this time
the idea of decay, the possibility
of durations less than forever will remain
a shadow on the edge of the dreamscape.
She's always in front and to the left, always
worried, her eyes don't pan from the grass
to the beagles, from the bay window
to the child trying to eat his fist, her eyes
question a spot just ahead as her mouth
opens and closes in rhythm with her gait,
as if walking's how she talks her body
into a covenant with the future. He
seems prepared to revert to his former life
as a balloon, to let his smile unhinge
and become as round as his body, a preface
to an eternity looking down
from heaven and touching the oceans
like a child caressing the frantic
pages of a coloring book. I've
read we're estranged from nature
and believe it standing in aisle 12
at the supermarket where everything's
bright and useful and impossible
to kill impossible to bury deep

in the land or shoot into space or ever
be rid of unlike you or me or your cherished
spouse disappearing this moment
at your elbow as they try to remember
if Dennis Weaver or Clint Eastwood played
the original Festus. So I made a pact
with my shoes to avoid aisle 12 and spend
more time at my window, spend 11
to 11:05 at my window because a part
of nature passes every day in the form
of their silent devotion. And it's not
like Hallmark says that they're one
body one soul one breath *my darling forever*
yours not like Wayne Newton
would have us believe in Vegas in a room
for nothing a night that love is a song
is a few words in German is a thin
mustache that makes the weak swoon: if
they're a number it's zero, perfect
clasp of nothing: if they comprise a song
it's so thin no one hears it, not even
a whisper, not even the rustling of a leaf:
if they're dying which of course
they are with great speed with stunning
expertise they are not dying
because there's always the face
of the other the presence of the other
this shadow behind this body
in front this couple who pass every day
saying nothing to each other I can hear
but of course between them passes an eloquence
not encumbered by breath not stunned
by the indecency of words.

—•—•—•—

When Swearing at the Carpeting's Not Enough

All this whistling and target practice is me
being chipper. If you don't pay attention to the tune
something mystical happens and there's music

despite your best intentions. If you insert a few
simple parts the semiautomatic loses all
inhibitions and will just prattle on in the direction

of the quarter-inch-thick steel chicken. My friend
burned the steel chicken free of a larger plate
in the manner of Michelangelo looking

at marble and seeing a body writhing inside. I learned
to whistle while queued for the bathroom
at St. Mary's and was slapped by a nun

who with thousands of nuns was married to a bigamous
God. By whistling long and hard I surround
my body with a hive of sharp distractions, I've found

the sound-making parts of my brain interfere
with the feeling-an-ass-when-I've-been-lied-to
center, which is right behind Wernicke's area, a little

patch of cortical matter that if injured makes language
a scramble of noise. Like whistling can be,
or machine-gun fire that makes a seizure at the end

of my arm, or how loud language becomes, a buzzing
of words when the thing said is not the thing
meant, deception sends my head to one room,

my soul ends up in a trunk at the bottom
of a lake trying to shake off the chains. I hit
nothing close to Bach with my breath, my hand shies

from the domestic grace of the chicken for the hill
behind, each bullet invents a cloud of dirt,
a little vanity of storm. Really the cure's

the silent walk to the chicken with an empty clip,
when we'll sit and admire the waltz between barley
and wind until my friend says something

about the underside of cars that sounds like teeth
shaken in a Yahtzee cup, a clamor I'll nod to
as you would when you have no intention

of bartering for the trinkets of Fira but open
your hand and let the bills unfold like a bird
after an hour of rest in the brutal migration.

—•—•—•—

CPR

Admired the swoon
of the junkie behind the sub-

shop door and his arms
fluttered

crane-wise at his side
when the buckling

knees and so
kissed him

with breath
disciplined his chest

and the stopped
moment of his heart

became the vassal
once more

of pious
needles

and my friend
big

as the moon
in face

laughed
I'd saved

a life in the sense
that killing

everyone
would open up

a lot
of space.

Book Report

I caught a sturgeon once
without bait. My uncle said
we were both stupid, one for believing
in a hook, the other for wading
shoeless into the Mississippi.
When he died, I didn't
wear underwear to the funeral
and reminded him with my thoughts
that I let the fish go, no butter
in a pan, no flesh-licked fingers
that night with Budweiser. Getting even
can be a very quiet thing done
without underwear. Some fish
are dogs that bark in bubbles
under water. The sturgeon
was a snow tire, all knobby
and grooved and notched, its nose
was long and it looked
at me in the same way I question
the mirror, I see flesh, I see hair
but beyond that a ferris wheel
and behind that a little boy
jumping up and down, trying to get
the horizon's attention. There are zero
sturgeon in the Mississippi now.
This is like saying there are no
Teds anymore, only worse. I've never
liked a Ted, there's Ted Turner
but I don't know him and wouldn't
take Jane Fonda's word. He owns
vast parts of several states but not
any sturgeon that live
in the Mississippi
because they don't, they did
for three hundred million years
without changing much
but have recently evolved
to death. The people who care about this
own too many Subarus, don't enjoy
Big Gulps as a rule and are prone

to announce their lactose
intolerance to waiters who don't
understand how the feast is prepared.
If more people with bulldozers cared
about the sturgeon, or those who own
malls, or those who crochet
portraits of Hoover at night to calm
their mind
from fidgety considerations
of the gold standard, imagine
the strength of this coalition,
the good they could do
by vacationing for a century
or two, vanishing
from the gear works of money, when tides
would heal, and the green things
that cling
and brown things that stalk
other brown things
would have a fighting chance, all any god
could ask. Did you know isinglass
comes from the bladder of the Russian
sturgeon? The correct answer to this
is not
for long. My uncle
has been dead for years. Where
is that fishing pole and hook? I write now
with coffee nearby and sunlight
on my hands. Without underwear, by the way,
though little good this does the sturgeon, a fish
I once knew as a thrash in amazed
hands.

—•—•—•—

Fairy Tale with Repetition

The Germans clothed him in a specially tailored, miniature SS uniform, which he wore when spraying bullets from his lordly perch on his pony.

—Hitler's Willing Executioners

Once upon a time a little boy
ate chocolate as he rode

a white pony. Licked chocolate
from his white fingers as he rode

a white pony. Wore a smart uniform
once upon a time, once

upon a century atop
a white pony. Ten years old

this little boy, called
my little cuttlefish, my little

ambassador of death. Once
upon a time in the Clothing Works

there lived one child, all
others harvested, one

little boy with a face
more like the moon every day, fatter

by chocolate,
and his fingers pudgier, fat

fingers holding a machine gun.
A machine gun all his own,

fat fingers licked
of chocolate, a white pony

in the Clothing Works, little
boy in a tiny

SS uniform, a Waffen
Jew, a ten-year-old

Jew with a pony, chocolate,
a machine gun to point

in the Clothing Works.
Little boy, little trigger.

Fat Jew killing skeletal
Jews, the shadow

Jews made to load
the little boy's gun, to kiss

the ass of his pony. Little boy,
white pony, chocolate,

machine gun, his mother
dead, fat finger

on little trigger, a little
boy, his dead mother, extra

chocolate that night, for
a week until they hanged

him, once upon a time
with a noose

placed by his own
fat hands.

—•—•—•—

Did I ever tell you about my love/hate relationship with confessional poetry?

Sometimes I leave my head in the other room.
Sometimes the other room is a few days
by horse away. I once told a man

I'd had a good time at the funeral,
which was true, not knowing the body
in the casket before it had ceased

to move and what with the sandwiches,
what with the woman to my left
smelling like she was the motive

of summer as she whispered the Polish names
from a novel in which no bad thing
happened. Usually bad things happen

in novels every chapter, this is how
narrative's advanced, a prince is born
and a prince gets dysentery and a prince

dies in a revolution with an appetite
for princes. As a child I held my breath
to break the knees of advancing narrative,

my face turned blue and body collapsed,
my parents looked at their little heap
of boy and loved me despite the evidence.

Even now you could ask that I imagine
a field and instead of poppies waving
blue heads I'd picture a tractor on fire,

smoke and a farmer standing back, resigned
with hands in pockets as if this too
is just a change of season. The other thing

I get wrong most of the time is caring
about people. For instance: recently blood
collected in my grandmother where blood

shouldn't, everything she said came out
like Jiffy Pop on the stove just before
the foil rips, people cried and the hospital

was a factory of indifference and I scurried
home to write a poem about death. This
is an indication that my head's not

in the other room but up my ass and that
my soul's in there with it. I don't mean
to care less about people than what

people do, and could lie and say
I've taken steps to increase my devotion
to the actual limbs that come off and hearts

that stop, so I will. The art
of confession's to focus attention on what's
confessed while leaving the secret

mutations untouched. I once put the hose
of a vacuum on my penis and turned it
on. Honesty makes me feel so clean.

—•—•—•—

What Would Freud Say?

Wasn't on purpose that I drilled
through my finger or the nurse
laughed. She apologized
three times and gave me a shot
of something that was a lusher
apology. The person
who drove me home
said my smile was a smeared
totem that followed
his body that night as it arced
over a cliff in a dream.
He's always flying
in his dreams and lands
on cruise ships or hovers
over Atlanta with an erection.
He put me to bed and the drugs
wore off and I woke
to cannibals at my extremities.
I woke with a sense
of what nails in the palms
might do to a spirit
temporarily confined to flesh.
That too was an accident
if you believe Judas
merely wanted to be loved.
To be loved by God,
Urban the Eighth
had heads cut off
that were inadequately
bowed by dogma. To be loved
by Blondie, Dagwood
gets nothing right
except the hallucinogenic
architecture of sandwiches.
He would have drilled
through a finger too
while making a case for books
on home repair and health.
Drilling through my finger's
not the dumbest thing

I've done. Second place
was approaching
a frozen gas-cap with lighter
in hand while thinking
heat melts ice and not
explosion kills asshole. First
place was passing
through a bedroom door
and removing silk that did not
belong to my wife.
Making a bookcase is not
the extent of my apology.
I've also been beaten up
in a bar for saying *huevos*
rancheros in a way
insulting to the patrons'
ethnicity. I've also lost
my job because lying
face down on the couch
didn't jibe with my employer's
definition of home
office. I wanted her to come
through the door on Sunday
and see the bookcase
she'd asked me to build
for a year and be impressed
that it didn't lean
or wobble even though
I've only leaned and often
wobbled. Now it's half
done but certainly
a better gift with its map
of my unfaithful blood.

—•—•—•—

A Little Science

Roosters fit the bill. Bucholz got some rooster heads, froze them and measured the rate at which they warmed up. Then he plucked them and repeated the process.

—from an article in *Scientific American*
about baldness in birds

If we skin the trustees the university will not
approve the Sports Psychology Center. Dancers'

toes sawed off, the ABT would look like the spawn
of Jerry Lewis and Martha Graham. Removing

the colon of the Speaker of the House without
consent or anesthesia would in no way

reduce interest in the job. Three pounds of six-
pound nails driven by a sixteen-pound

hammer into the two-pound skull of the next
Jehovah's Witness who assails your door

would prove nothing but you'd do it anyway. Though
deveining an adult male means his certain

death, this should not affect funding of the project,
Senator. A laptop computer with modem and CD-ROM

could fit in a womb, redefining the term *home office.*
If you look closely at the patella you realize

there's sufficient surface area to drill
and tap for an eyebolt, for what purpose

the private sector can better decide. By inducing
blindness in painters by physical or chemical means,

and asking them to paint the London Bridge over
and over, we can determine to what extent Monet

was artistically motivated or just bored. Remove
a pituitary: reduce it to paste with pestle and mortar:

add Fruit Loops, a dash of Brute, some aloe and pesto
and WD-40: treat with Uranium-235: feed it back

to the subject with a Fred Flintstone spoon: ask
if they prefer the original or touring cast of *Cats:*

present the results in *Nature:* apply for NIS grant.
Go home. Kiss spouse. Read paper. Pet dog.

—•—•—•—

Once a green sky

A deer was on Linwood and I asked the forest
to come and retrieve her, curl its slow hammers
around our houses and decipher brick into scraps
of clay. My hardest wishes are for and against

ourselves, delicate locusts, ravenous flowers
with an appetite for even the breaths
between the spaces. Say you are alone. Pretend
everyone emulates you. Imagine if alone

the idea of the conversion van, the strong touch
of burrito wafting from the bodega, never
germinated in the cavernous brain. Hands
are no more clever than kneading dough,

the weapon of choice is sleep, the gods we adore
eat their own ribs, supplicant postures
of apology break out simultaneously in each
cabin and in exactly the same way. Impossible, OK,

move on. What if instead I owned one TV
and shared it with you on weekends, Lucille Ball
eating chocolate after chocolate as we laugh
in tribal reflex. If there was just one car

we touched the third Sunday of each month,
licked the leather seats, turned the engine
over and ran behind the bushes, terrified
at the growling dog we'd created, could this be

enough? There's a surprise in all flesh, this
is the purpose of eyes, to find and convey shock.
The deer and I faced as mistakes of context,
errors of intention, and she shot into the same

confusion one street over, we are saints
of replication, my house is your house, my
pierced navel your erection, the deer sniffed
for the green mist, thrashed through an archipelago

of false indicators, islands of shrubs that lasted
five paces, ten breaths, until she ran
into the mouth of a Saturn. From skulls I know
the architecture of her bones, lacy nostrils,

the torsion grooves of ligaments, just as kissing
a shoulder I have faith in the cup
and ball that work the joint, making it curl
into pleasure. I can't shrug gravity, the *Holy*

Spirit Force, but if possible would dream
silks of what contains us, the habit to make,
to adore the crystal chandelier
whose frail music each day is a dirge

for a hundred species. What if the forest
followed the deer, not into death but through
my living room, what if the rain ate my den
and you and I, unrolling a set of blueprints,

realized the sky is aspiration enough? Or if you
and I, reaching for a vowel, for the last
piece of coal on the stack, gave
silence, gave the eventual diamond back.

—•—•—•—

Acknowledgments

I thank the editors of the following publications for publishing my poetry:

Boulevard: "Rapture," "The Party," "When Swearing at the Carpeting's Not Enough," "Whither Thou Goest"

Chelsea: "Fairy Tale with Repetition," "Monograph on the Walkers"

Cream City Review: "What Would Freud Say?"

Green Mountains Review: "Critique of Pure Unreason"

Indiana Review: "33," "Magic"

The Journal: "Sorting the Entanglements"

Kenyon Review: "How Origami was Invented," "What Fine Kindling the Homeless Make"

Massachusetts Review: "Everyday Commerce," "To the Moon, Alice"

Michigan Quarterly Review: "Neither Here nor There"

Missouri Review: "Book Report"

North American Review: "A Small Blasphemy"

Ploughshares: "Once a green sky"

Poetry: "Ha'ish hu ha'ish"

Poetry Northwest: "A Little Science," "Season of Levitation"

Quarterly West: "Vagina canticle"

Shenandoah: "CPR"

Southern Review: "An incidental report on my grandmother's divinity," "Finally I Buy X-ray Glasses," "Headline: CLEAN-SWEEP CLEARS PARKS & GRATES"

Third Coast: "Did I ever tell you about my love/hate relationship with confessional poetry?," *"Harms Way"*

Water/Stone: "Pol Pot's Class Reunion"

—•••—

"Birth of a Saint," "Cross Town," "Perpetual Resurrection," and "The Subjects' Exodus" were part of a chapbook entitled *Defenestration,* which appeared in *Black Warrior Review.*

"What Would Freud Say" appeared in *Best American Poetry 1999.*

"Once a green sky" was reprinted on *Poetry Daily.*

Thanks also to the NEA for a fellowship that allowed me to complete this book.